Music by the Masters

Compiled, Edited and Annotated by Russell E. Lanning

Alfred Music
P.O. Box 10003
Van Nuys, CA 91410-0003
alfred.com

ISBN-10: 0-7692-3953-6
ISBN-13: 978-0-7692-3953-8

Dedicated to the inspiring
teachings of Calvin B. Cady

Contents
of Music by the Masters

Preface

INTRODUCTORY REMARKS

A long line of musical thought is better than several small thoughts.
The above principle is the basis of the editing in this volume.

Stating this in another way, we might say that analysis is necessary but a synthetic understanding must be obtained if one is to play with authority; for analysis breaks down while synthesis creates a whole from the small pieces.

Only the experienced artist or the few students with talent who are fortunate enough to be associated with the finest teachers play with any idea of musical line. It is this one great principle that guides the great performers and orchestra leaders. These good musicians may be likened to a person standing on a mountain top and looking down seeing the whole world stretching out beautifully before them. The others play as though they were hidden away in some remote corner and unable to see the world about them.

The system of phrasing used in this volume makes it possible for any qualified student to understand and play these classics like an experienced artist; for each number is so treated that by observing the brackets, one can see at a glance the relationship of the parts and the broad, beautiful sweet of the musical ideas.

In speech we find principal clauses, subordinate clauses and independent clauses. In music we find identical groups which in this volume are indicated by brackets.

THE LANNING PHRASING SYSTEM

All phrases are either dependent or independent.
A dependent phrase is one which requires two or more phrases to complete the musical thought.
Such phrases are indicated in this volume by the following brackets:

Examples of dependent phrases

> Sonatina in G by Beethoven, page 9 - line 1, measures 1 to 4
> Sonatina in F by Beethoven, page 12 - line 1, measures 1 to 4
> The Merry Farmer by Schumann, page 14 - beginning to third bar, also last note on line 2 to next to last note on second measure of line 3.

An independent phrase is one which by itself makes a complete musical statement.
Such phrases are indicated in this volume by the following brackets:

Examples of independent phrases

> Soldiers March by Schumann, page 6 - first eight measures - second eight measures.
> Arietta In A by Haydn, page 16 - first two lines.
> Minuet In G by Bach, page 17 - first eight measures.
> Little Dance in F by Haydn, page 21 - first two lines.
> Two Ecossaises by Schubert, page 20 - all of first line.

All phrases whether dependent or independent are divided into three types: — harmonic - rhythmic - metric.
A harmonic phrase is one which usually ends at a harmonically satisfied resolution.

Examples of harmonic phrases

> Theme and Variation by Beethoven, page 25 - first note, measure 4.
> Prelude No. 2 by Bach, page 52 - measure 4 and first note at line 3.
> Solfeggietto by Bach, page 42 - first note of third measure and fifth note of fifth measure.
> The Little Reaper's Song by Schumann, page 28 - end of measure 2 and end of measure 4.

Remarks — In most of the works of Bach, the harmonic pattern and harmonic phrase are the only ones used. These groups change their form and length continually thus helping make music more interesting.

A metric phrase is one which ends after two or more measures at a bar.

Examples of metric phrases

> Sonata in C by Mozart, page 68 - measures 12, 15 17.
> Prelude Op. 28, No. 6 by Chopin, page 57 - measure 8.
> Venetian Boat Song by Mendelssohn, page 60, measure 6.
> Courante by Handel, page 64 - line 3 - third bar

Remarks — It is very seldom that one finds the metric phrase in good music of the nineteenth century (Romantic Period). Schumann, Mendelssohn, Brahms, Tschaikowsky seldom ended phrases at a bar; in other words they did not hear nor think metrically. Grieg, on the other hand, composed mostly on Norwegian Folk Themes which are almost all formed metrically. His music is thus not as highly rated as that which is conceived harmonically and where harmony controls the phrasing.

A rhythmic phrase is one which ends at the end of a rhythmic pattern and which is composed of two or more rhythmic patterns.

Examples of dependent phrases

> Horseman's Song by Schumann; page 72 - end of line 1 - third measure - line 3.
> Two Ecossaises by Schubert, page 20 - measure 4 and measure 12.

Remarks — Rhythmic phrasing is used in the dance forms. Pure rhythmic phrasing is phrasing which does not depend on harmonic satisfaction for its resolution. Pure rhythmic phrasing is found in the dances of Handel, Bach, Beethoven, Mozart, Chopin and in some of Mendelssohn. This does not mean that these composers used pure rhythmic phrasing only. In the second section of Beethoven's "Minuet in G," the rhythmic pattern changes to harmonic; the same holds true for all great music which is made interesting by the composer's change of pattern.

A harmonic - rhythmic phrase is a phrase in which the harmony runs parallel to and ends at the same point of satisfaction as the rhythmic pattern.

Examples of harmonic-rhythmic phrases

> Arietta in A by Haydn, page 16 - measures 4 and 8.
> Allegro by Mozart, page 19 - end of first line, sixth measure of line 2.
> Wild Horseman by Schumann, page 27 - end of line 1 and at double bar.

A harmonic-metric phrase is a phrase in which the harmony ends in satisfaction at a bar along with the metric phrase.

Examples of harmonic-metric phrases

> Musette by Bach, page 8 - all phrases.
> Grandmother's Minuet by Grieg, page 22 - at bar 4 of line 1 and at bar 4 of line 2.
> Northern Song by Schumann, page 26 - end of first line.

Finally, it should also be noted that all phrases whether harmonic, rhythmic or metric and harmonic-rhythmic or harmonic-metric are herein indicated as dependent or independent phrases *only*.

When music is heard and understood in this manner, then the bars and measures become merely an aid to keeping time as they were only meant to be originally and one's playing becomes musically smoother; crescendos will be held to their limit and diminuendos will be smoother and help with intelligence based on an absolute knowledge, not mere feeling.

MUSCULAR REACTIVE PHRASE

This original term is given to groups of legato notes denoted by a slur with a dot at the end. The muscular reactive phrase is usually composed of two notes, the first one being the stronger. In playing such groups, the experienced artist drops his arm and wrist with weight on the first note followed by a natural rebound up on the following note. Such groups are the most disregarded of all musical or technical problems encountered by students.

The term "Muscular Reactive Phrase" is well suited to these groups as they are a natural technical phenomena; for the rebound on the last note is a reaction caused by an opposite force on the preceding note.

Examples of Muscular Reactive Phrases

> Allegro in B flat by Mozart, page 19 — all of R.H. in measure 1 - also R.H. in measure 1 on line 2.

Remarks — The inexperienced student whose technic is not properly developed does not react naturally or rebound from accents or points of stress or pressure. These exacting markings have been placed most carefully and will be found as a great aid to better progress.

HARMONIC LINE

Many musicians use the term "Melodic Line." This is a very loose and indefinite term for pure melodic thought is not possible mentally nor theoretically. All tone has natural harmonies, therefore "Harmonic Line" is the one great controlling musical factor used in this volume.

Harmonic Line controls all interpretation and in most of the dance forms it may be observed that although the dance may be composed on a particular rhythmic pattern, harmonic line has final say and in some places causes a change in the original rhythmic pattern as in the second part of Beethoven's Minuet in F, page 59.

RUSSELL E. LANNING.

Soldier's March

An excellent example for the use of prepared touch. Prepared touch is accomplished mentally and physically by placing the fingers in contact with the succeeding notes during the rest period between notes.

Edited by
Russell B. Lanning

SCHUMANN

EL2543

Minuet in G

Edited by
Russell B. Lanning

PEZOLD

EL2543

Musette

Edited by
Russell E. Lanning

UNKNOWN

Allegro

Sonatina in G

One of two sonatinas written when Beethoven was a child. Use very
little pedal.

Edited by
Russell B. Lanning

BEETHOVEN

EL2543

ROMANZE

Sonatina in F

Edited by
Russell E. Lunning

The phrasing in this number which is the second of two sonatinas
written by Beethoven when a child, should be carefully noted.

BEETHOVEN

Allegro assai

The Merry Farmer

The chords in the right hand provide an excellent example of prepared touch.
Starting with the note C in each hand in the middle section, have the pupil play
the melody alone and think (not play) the accompaniment. Then play melody
with the accompaniment subdued and all staccato.

Edited by
Russell E. Lanning

SCHUMANN

Bring out the Left Hand melody

espressivo

Italian Folk Song

Edited by
Russell E. Lanning

An excellent example of Italian Folk Music. It is simple in its structure and melodic content. It is gay and light. In order to achieve this light effect, be sure to play the staccatos as marked.

TSCHAIKOWSKY

EL2543

Arietta in A

An excellent study for practice of legato touch with clean, bell-like tones in the right hand. The left hand must be played lightly and cleanly without overlapping of tones.

Edited by
Russell E. Lanning

HAYDN

Minuet in G

Edited by
Russell E. Lanning

This is a good example of the original form of the minuet, which during
the 17th and 18th century began on the first beat. Later the minuet in
the 19th century started on the third beat.(See Beethoven Minuet in G,
page 59)

BACH

Polonaise

The Polonaise is a lively dance. In order to create a brilliant effect,
be sure to play all staccato notes brightly.

Edited by
Russell E. Lanning

WOLFGANG AMADEUS MOZART

Allegro in B flat

Ordinarily musical ideas are expressed in multiples of two measures
(2-4-8-16-32). In this number we have the unusual element of a six
measure phrase, beautifully combined with the standard eight measure
phrase.

*Edited by
Russell E. Lanning*

MOZART

Two Ecossaises

These two Scotch Dances should be played with little pedal, good accent and without any change in tempo

Edited by
Russell E. Lanning

SCHUBERT

Little Dance in F

This dance is in the style of a minuet. Use a light touch and little pedal.

Edited by
Russell E. Lanning

HAYDN

EL2543

Grandmother's Minuet

A splendid staccato study. Stress all accents and watch all pianissimos.

Edited by
Russell E. Lanning

GRIEG

Allegretto grazioso e leggierissimo

Ecossaise in G

This is a Scotch Dance. Play happily and watch all the accents.

Edited by
Russell E. Lanning

BEETHOVEN

EL2543

Theme And Variation

It will be noted that this number comprises many slurred groups of two
notes. These groups begin with a slightly accented note or chord which
should be connected to a following note. In executing these groups the hand
drops on the first note and the reaction of the drop causes an up-thrust
on the following note. In this volume we call these Technical Reactive Groups.

Edited by
Russell B. Lanning

BEETHOVEN

Andante, Quasi Allegretto

EL2543

Northern Song

An excellent pedal study. Be sure to play the hands exactly together.
The right hand should be a bit stronger.

Edited by
Russell E. Lanning

SCHUMANN

52

Wild Horseman

The accompaniment figure should be practiced many times so that it becomes automatic. The player should feel the music in groups of four measures.

*Edited by
Russell B. Lanning*

SCHUMANN

The Little Reaper's Song

The two voices in the right hand should be learned separately so that the continuity and values of all notes are realized. All notes are legato, except when marked staccato.

Edited by Russell E. Lanning

SCHUMANN

Non troppo allegro

Minuet in C

Like all minuets of the nineteenth century, this one starts on the third
count but the first count must be accented a little.

Edited by
Russell E. Lanning

BEETHOVEN

EL2543

Hunter's Song

In the music of Beethoven (Grieg also) the *sf* sign should especially be
noted. Where such signs appear the student should use a sudden loud touch.

Edited by
Russell E. Lanning

BEETHOVEN

Minuet in C

Edited by
Russell E. Lanning

This minuet is constructed with harmonic-rhythmic patterns; that is, the rhythmic idea which begins on the third count of each two measures and ends on the second count of the following measures may also be considered as a harmonic idea with each ending being a complete or a semi harmonic cadence, with groups of such ideas forming the rhythmic harmonic line. Pedal should be used carefully and all technical legato-staccato groups should be clearly executed.

HAYDN

Scherzo
From Fourth Sonatina

This number should be played lightly and with exceptional attention given to clean precise finger activity.

Edited by
Russell B. Lanning

HAYDN

Waltz in A minor No. 1

A good study in legato. Note the fingering in the octave passages. They are also legato.

Edited by
Russell E. Lanning

SCHUBERT

EL2543

First Loss

A study for legato, tone production and for the use of rubato

SCHUMANN

Edited by
Russell E. Lanning

Non Allegro

Waltz in B♭

To be played in a real lusty fashion like an old German beer garden dance.

Edited by
Russell E. Lanning

SCHUBERT

EL2543

Waltz

This favorite of so many students must be played with careful attention
to all accents and staccato notes.

Edited by
Russell E. Lanning

GRIEG

Allegro moderato

Allegro in F major

Watch all dynamic markings carefully and be sure to hold all crescendos
to their full length. Make all staccato notes crisp and clear.

HAYDN

Edited by
Russell E. Lanning

Sarabande

Play solidly with each key fully depressed.

Edited by
Russell E. Lanning

HANDEL

Lento non troppo

VARIATION

Gigue

A lively dance. Play evenly and without pedal.

Edited by
Russell E. Lanning

HANDEL

Solfeggietto

Edited by
Russell E. Lanning

Study the tonal ranges throughout the piece. The most flawless, technical
execution will be of no avail without proper dynamics.

BACH

Sailor's Song

This piece must be played with great depth of tone.

Edited by
Russell E. Lanning

GRIEG

Phantasietanz

This number should be played almost wildly but with careful thought given to pedal and the rhythmic-harmonic pattern, which starts on the fourth count of each measure.

Edited by
Russell E. Lanning

SCHUMANN

Bagatelle

Play with strict regard for accent and staccato.

Edited by
Russell E. Lanning

BEETHOVEN

Risoluto

Prelude in E Minor

This prelude should be played very legato. All tones should be sustained
by the use of the pedal which should change at each change of harmony.

Edited by
Russell E. Lanning

CHOPIN

espress.

alarg.

p

legato

stretto

f

rit.

a tempo

dim.

p

alarg.

smorz.

pp

rit.

Prelude № I

Edited by
Russell E. Lanning

This prelude should be played as one long phrase and with steady tonal growth until the pattern changes at the ninth measure.

J. S. BACH

Prelude № II

A fine study in weight legato playing in which great opportunity for
dynamic contrast is afforded.

Edited by
Russell E. Lanning

J. S. BACH

Little Prelude in D minor

Should be played with very little pedal and with little weight.

Edited by
Russell E. Lanning

J. S. BACH

Little Prelude In F Major

Edited by
Russell E Lanning

Constructed on a motive consisting of four notes. Pedal should be
used sparingly.

J. S. BACH

Allegretto

Little Prelude Nº I
from Six Little Preludes

The mordents in this prelude should be played in exact time, just as
they are written.

Edited by
Russell E. Lanning

J.S. BACH

EL2543

Prelude

Play with broad tone and flexible wrists.

Edited by
Russell E. Lanning

CHOPIN
Op. 28, No. 20

Prelude (B Minor)

Edited by
Russell E. Lanning

Use close finger action in R.H. with arm weight. L.H. should be very sustained.

CHOPIN
Op. 28, No. 6

Lento assai

p sotto voce

sostenuto

p

Edited by
Russell E. Lanning

Prelude in A

Be sure to bring out the upper notes in the R.H. and keep them
as legato as possible.

CHOPIN
Op.28, No.7

Andantino

p dolce

Minuet in G

In the double note portions, it may be desirable to study the upper notes
alone in order to feel the legato quality of the melody.

Edited by
Russell B. Lanning

BEETHOVEN

Venetian Boat Song

This number (a type of composition originated by Mendelssohn) is exceptionally valuable for the study of legato. The left hand should be subdued, yet all tones should be played deeply into the keys.

Edited by
Russell E. Lanning

MENDELSSOHN

EL2543

Valse Sentimentale

Edited by
Russell E. Lanning

Written as a dance in the early waltz style the tempo should therefore be
steady and the first note of each measure should be slightly held. Do not
staccato this first note.

SCHUBERT

Air

Edited by
Russell E. Lanning

To be played very fast and with carefully clipped staccatos while
the R.H. is legato.

HANDEL

Courante

Edited by
Russell E. Lanning

To be played in strict tempo and with careful regard for all phrasing and staccato.

HANDEL

Piu vivo

Waltz in C

Edited by
Russell E. Lanning

A remarkable tonal growth takes place in this number. Save your energy
for the fortissimo near the end. Do not anticipate the climax.

SCHUBERT

Waltz in A Minor No.2

A good study for a large hand, using octave chords and open octaves.
Must be played with freedom with arm relaxed from the shoulder.

Edited by
Russell E. Lanning

SCHUBERT

Allegro non troppo

Sonata No.1 in C

This is one of the most famous sonatas of Mozart. Play lightly and
evenly. Runs should be practiced with hands alone until freedom is at-
tained.

Edited by
Russell E. Lanning

MOZART

Horseman's Song

This number is supposed to describe the clatter of the hoofs of a galloping horse. To create this effect, be sure to release staccato notes quickly.

Edited by
Russell E. Lanning

SCHUMANN

Opera Memories

Observe all groupings, especially contrasting staccato and legato notes. In the
second section on line three, both hands should be played with equal weight.

Edited by
Russell E. Lanning

SCHUMANN

EL2543

Perfect Happiness

Edited by
Russell E. Lanning

The staccato notes have been added only to aid in holding notes in upper voice.

SCHUMANN

EL2543

D.C.

Of Foreign Lands and People

Edited by
Russell E. Lanning

The staccato notes which have been added to the usual legato accompaniment may be termed technical staccato When used with pedal these notes remain resonant and aid the player to hold the upper voice legato.

SCHUMANN

Melody legato

Fur Elise

Edited by
Russell E. Lanning

This popular piece contains every type of phrase group; the harmonic
phrase predominating. Notice the many staccato notes added as an aid
to clean playing, so that hands do not overlap when playing at the cor-
rect tempo.

BEETHOVEN

Poco moto

Knight Rupert

Edited by
Russell E. Lanning

Knight Rupert is a mythical European character like Santa Claus.
This number should be played happily and with great zest.

SCHUMANN

Folk Song

Edited by
Russell E. Lanning

As in all of Greig's music this rhythmical number should be played
with regard for sudden contrasts of tone and accent.

GRIEG

Allegro con moto

EL2543

Arietta

Edited by
Russell E. Lanning

The melody is all important, while the accompaniment should be played
quietly with no overlapping of notes.

GRIEG

Poco Andante e sostenuto

Prelude

No. 1 from Well Tempered Clavichord

May be played without pedal. A splendid study for finger control.

Edited by
Russell E. Lanning

BACH

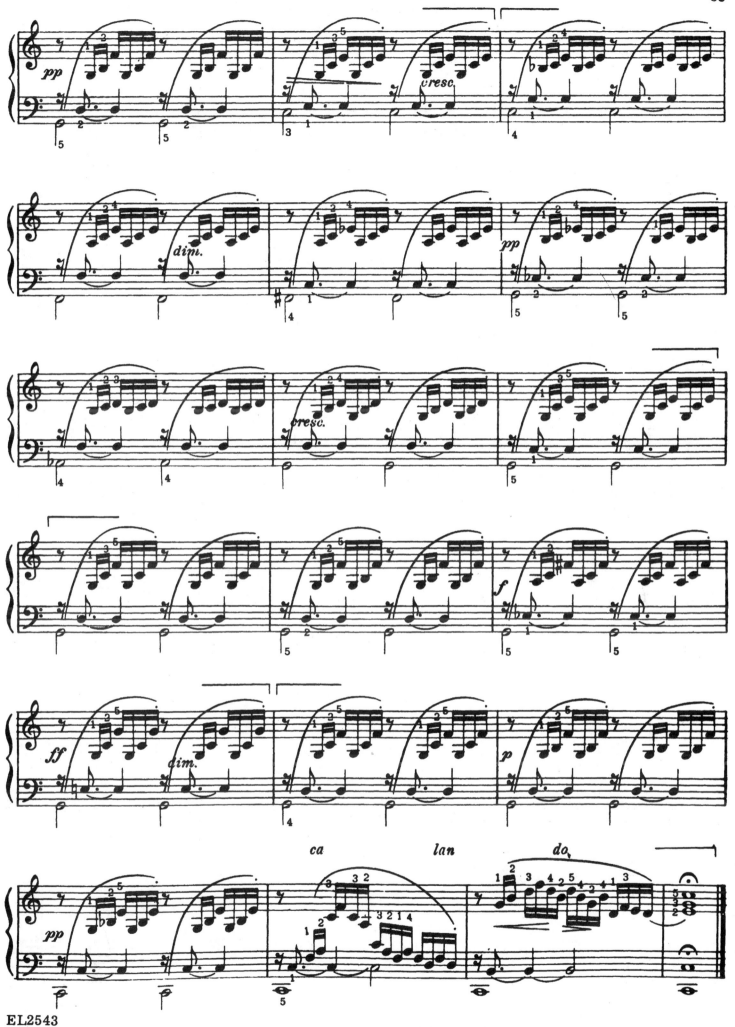

Mazurka
(Op. 68 No. 3)

Do not use much rubato or rit. and keep the accompaniment even.

Edited by
Russell E. Lanning

CHOPIN

Allegro, ma non troppo

Mazurka
(Op. 67 No. 2)

Edited by
Russell E. Lanning

CHOPIN

Keep the R.H. legato where marked and the L.H. swinging with the aid
of the pedal in legato — crisp staccato groups.

Cantabile

Mazurka
(Op.67 No.4)

Edited by
Russell E. Lanning

Keep the L.H. steady. All rubato effects should be accomplished in the R.H.

CHOPIN

Moderato animato

Mazurka

Edited by
Russell E. Lanning

This Mazurka should be kept going. Do not use too much rubato nor too much ritard, and keep the accompaniment as even as possible.

CHOPIN
Op.67 No.3

Allegro

Mazurka
(Op. 7 No. 2)

Edited by
Russell E. Lanning

Notice how many times the L.H. is played staccato, while the R.H. is legato
in the A minor section. Notice the legato L.H. section in the begining and
ending of the A major section.

CHOPIN

Vivo, ma non troppo (♩=160)

EL2543

D.C.al Fine.

Adagio

Edited by
Russell E. Lanning

A rarely heard and beautiful example of two part writing. All phrasing is harmonic in this number.

BACH